Contents

Introduction

The dictionary describes an architect as "a person whose profession is to design buildings and direct their construction." But people are not the only architects in the world! Human architects are at the end of a long line of remarkable builders. We are actually the most recent builders on the planet. Millions of years before the first human built the first building, animals were building their homes. Some even built large "cities."

Animal architects do not build from drawings or blueprints. Rather, they build from plans that exist only in their brains. Their building plans have been passed from parent to offspring over the course of millions of years.

Meet the Animal Architects

This book will introduce you to just a few of the many fascinating animal architects in the world today. You will discover how they design both resting and living spaces, cradles in which to raise their young, and places to gather and store their food. Most important, you will see how their buildings help them survive in the natural world.

Each group of animals has its own unique methods of construction. Clams, snails, and a few of their relatives build some of the most beautiful structures in all of nature. Their empty homes are the seashells you find at the beach.

Bees, ants, termites, and wasps are among the most interesting architects in the world of insects. They work alone or in large groups to build some remarkably complex homes. Some nests grow larger than a grocery bag and can include five or six stories, with entrances and exits throughout.

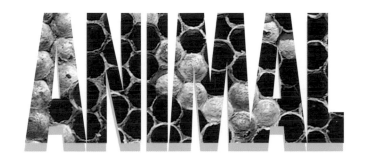

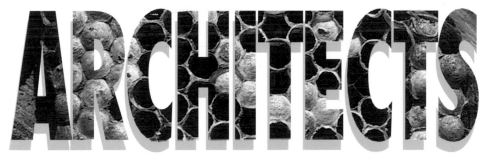

ANIMAL ARCHITECTS

How **INSECTS**
Build Their Amazing Homes

W. Wright Robinson

B L A C K B I R C H   P R E S S ,   I N C .

W O O D B R I D G E ,   C O N N E C T I C U T

Acknowledgement
The author thanks Dr. Mark W. Moffett and Dr. Harry B. Moore for
their help in reviewing all or part of the material for this book.

Dedication
To my father, for being the fine man that he is.

Published by Blackbirch Press, Inc.
260 Amity Road
Woodbridge, CT 06525

©1999 by Blackbirch Press, Inc.
First Edition

e-mail: staff@blackbirch.com
Web site: www.blackbirch.com

Printed in Hong Kong

10 9 8 7 6 5 4 3 2 1

Library of Congress Cataloging-in-Publication Data
Robinson, W. Wright.
How insects build their amazing homes/W. Wright Robinson. — 1st ed.
    p.   cm. — (Animal architects)
   Includes bibliographical references and index.
   Summary: Describes how termites, wasps, bees, and ants live and work together in
organized colonies that build large, complex homes.
    ISBN 1-56711-375-3 (library binding : alk. paper)
    1. Bees—Nests—Juvenile literature. 2. Ants—Nests—Juvenile literature.
3. Termites—Nests—Juvenile literature. 4. Wasps—Nests—Juvenile literature.
[1. Bees—Nests. 2. Ants—Nests. 3. Termites—Nests. 4. Wasps—Nests. 5. Insects—
Habits and behavior.]
I. Title. II. Series.
QL565.2.R635   1999
595.79'1564—dc21

98-47975
CIP
AC

1/4/01

Spiders are magnificent architects whose small, often hard-to-find silk homes are every inch as complex and amazing as the larger homes of birds and mammals. Some spiders actually build trapdoors to hide themselves and ambush prey. Others construct beautiful square silken boxes as traps, while they hang suspended in the air!

Birds are another group of remarkable architects. Most people think a bird's nest is simply made of sticks and grass in the shape of a bowl. While this shape describes some nests, it by no means describes them all. Some, like the edible saliva nests of the swiftlets, for example, are quite unusual. In fact, our human ancestors may have learned to weave, sew, and make clay pots from watching winged architects build their nests!

The constructions of mammals are some of the grandest on Earth. Mammals are thinking animals. They can learn from their experiences and mistakes. Each time one of these animals builds a new home, it may be constructed a little differently, a little faster, and a little better.

I hope that you will enjoy reading these books. I also hope that, from them, you will learn to appreciate and respect the incredible builders of the animal world—they are the architects from whom we have learned a great deal about design and construction. They are also the architects who will continue to inspire and enlighten countless generations still to come.

W. Wright Robinson

About Insects

There are more types of insects in the world than there are types of animals and plants combined. No one knows exactly how many there are, but more than 800,000 kinds, or species of insects, have already been found. Each year, many new insects are discovered and added to the list. Some scientists believe that there could be a total of more than 10 million species of insects sharing planet Earth with us!

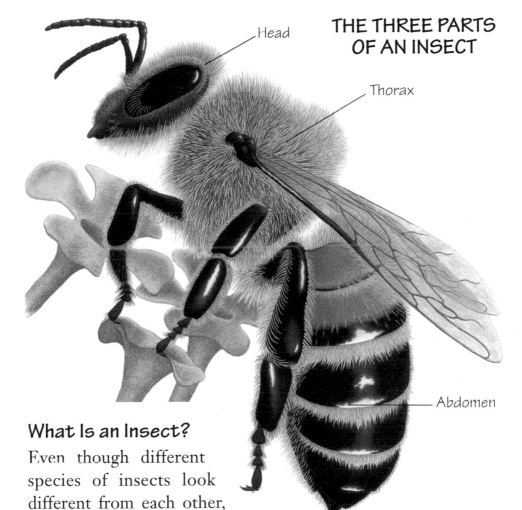

Head

THE THREE PARTS
OF AN INSECT

Thorax

Abdomen

What Is an Insect?

Even though different species of insects look different from each other, they are alike in many ways. Although their bodies may be different shapes and colors, all insects are relatively small. They range in length from 1/100 inch (0.2 millimeters) to 13 inches (330 millimeters).

All insects' bodies have three sections: head, thorax (chest), and abdomen. A single pair of feelers, called antennae, are attached to an insect's head, and three pairs of legs are attached to the thorax. Insects are the only animals that have all of these characteristics.

Dead and rotting wood makes ideal building material for many insects.

Where Do Insects Live?

Insects are found all over the world. They live in deserts, forests, grassy fields—and even in very cold places near the North and South poles. Some insects spend all or part of their lives in freshwater ponds, rivers, and streams. A few can even live in salty ocean water.

Termites, wasps, bees, and ants are some of the most social insects. Many of these animals live and work together in well-organized colonies that build large, complex homes. Even the bees and wasps that live and work alone are often remarkable builders.

Insect buildings can be found in and on the ground, or high in trees. Their buildings may be homes for an entire colony, or nurseries for young insects as they develop into adults. Termites, wasps, bees, and ants build their structures with mud, grass, wax, or wood, or almost any other type of material available.

THE TWO KINDS OF METAMORPHOSIS

From Egg to Adult:

Insects begin their lives inside eggs. Once they hatch and leave the eggs, their bodies gradually change shape until they become fully developed adults. This process of change is called metamorphosis.

The metamorphosis of an insect can be either complete or incomplete. If the metamorphosis is complete, the change to each stage of development is very distinct. If the metamorphosis is incomplete, the change is more gradual.

Grasshoppers, for example, experience an incomplete metamorphosis. Wasps, ants, and bees undergo a complete metamorphosis. These two processes are illustrated in the drawings on this page.

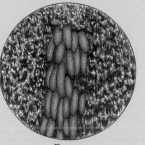

Eggs

Egg hatches into larva

Nymph

Larva

Nymph

Mature larva

Nymph

Pupa

Adult

Adult

Incomplete
Metamorphosis

Complete
Metamorphosis

Termites

In many parts of the world, termites are very well known for the damage they can cause to wooden buildings, furniture, fence posts, and utility poles. They also destroy paper products, such as books, maps, and many kinds of fabrics. Termites are not entirely bad, however. They feed on, and tunnel through, dead trees. As they do this, they help the dead wood to decompose. Gradually, the dead wood changes back into the minerals that living plants need to grow.

There are more than 3,000 different known species of termites in the world. Most of these insects live in warm, tropical climates, where they build some of the most fascinating homes in the animal kingdom.

The Houses That Termites Build

Termite homes, called nests or termitaria (ter–my–TARY–a), are found in many different shapes and sizes. Some termites tunnel through the wood they eat to make dwelling places. Others use soil to build enormous, rock-hard homes that can weigh several tons.

These architectural marvels are not built by just one or two termites working alone. Termites live and work together in groups called colonies. Depending on the species of termite, a single colony may consist of hundreds, thousands, or even millions of insects. Each colony, however, begins with only two termites—a king and a queen.

The large black clumps on this dead tree in Mexico are actually termite nests.

Starting the Nest

The king and queen build a small nest in the ground, in dry wood, or in damp, rotting wood (the location of the nest depends upon the species). Once the nest is prepared, the king and queen mate. After a few weeks, the female begins laying small batches of eggs. Both parents work to keep the eggs clean and care for them until they hatch.

After the eggs hatch, the parents must feed the young termites, called nymphs, for several weeks until the newborn insects are able to feed themselves. The queen continues laying eggs. When the first group of young termites is able to work, they take over the parents' job of cleaning and caring for the new eggs. As more and more eggs hatch, the number of termites in the colony increases rapidly, and the nest is made larger.

Within a well-organized colony, there are three classes of termites: the royal pair, the soldiers, and the workers. The royal pair, the king and queen who founded the colony, produce most of the young. The soldier termites defend the colony against attack—usually guarding against their number-one enemy, the ants. The workers expand the nest, and find food and water to feed the soldiers, the newly hatched nymphs, and the king and queen.

Above: A Nasuties king (top) and queen (large in middle) in a nest.
Below: Termite nymphs (white) and workers scamper through the twisted maze of their nest.

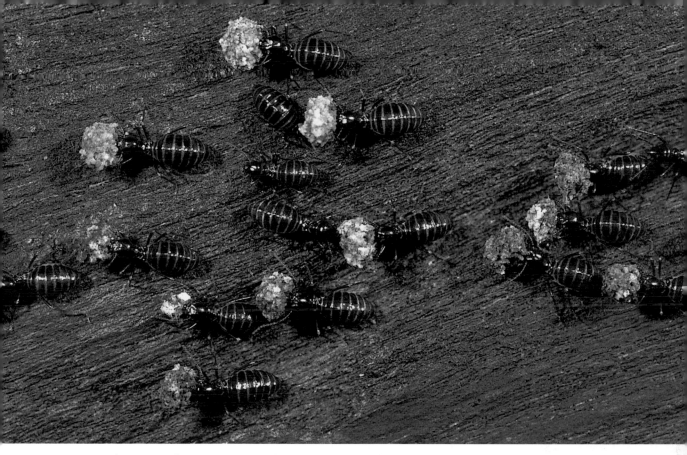

A team of termites on a log carries wood pulp to their nest.

Edible Houses

Some of the most destructive "house-eating" termites in parts of Asia, Europe, and the United States, build their nests in the darkness of cool, moist soil below the surface of the ground. These underground, or subterranean, termites do not, however, just crawl up to a house and start eating the wood from the floor to the roof.

As the colony grows, the workers must enlarge the nest and find enough food to feed all the other hungry termites. Each day, the workers tunnel through the soil in search of food. For them, wood is food—it does not matter if it is a tree or the floors, walls, or furniture of a house.

Strong jaws enable termites to turn wood and mud into sturdy building materials for a home.

When the workers find a solid piece of wood, they tunnel inside it with their sharp, powerful jaws and begin to eat. Subterranean termites remain safely hidden inside the wood while they feed. As they eat their way out toward the surface, they leave a paper-thin layer of the wood in place, keeping themselves well hidden. By working quietly out of sight, an army of termites from an underground nest can attack a house without ever being seen or heard.

Tunnels made of soil or wood protect termites as they travel between their food source and their nest.

If you look at the end of a freshly cut log, you will see light and dark rings in the wood. The light rings form in the spring when a tree gets plenty of water and sunlight and grows fast. When subterranean termites enter a piece of wood, they usually eat the light-colored wood first because it is softer. During the hot, dry summer months, when a tree cannot always get the water it needs, the wood grows slowly, forming the dark rings. The termites leave this dark, firm wood in place to form walls in the "upstairs dining room" of their nest. To reach the next ring of soft, light wood, they cut small doorways through the dark-wood walls.

Underground termites can also eat wood that is not touching the ground. These little architects build covered highways, called shelter tubes, over bricks, stones, concrete, or metal, in order to get from the ground to a piece of wood. To construct these tubes, a worker uses its jaws to carry a tiny bit of soil or wood to the "building site."

The worker positions the material, and then adds a drop of its glue-like waste to hold the material firmly in place. Then, the worker goes off to find another piece of soil or wood. If only one termite were working alone, the tube would be built very slowly. In a termite colony, however, hundreds or even thousands of termites are working together, and the job goes much faster.

After the tube is built, the workers can move safely between their nest and the wood. They must return every few days to the moist soil of their underground nest to replace the water that has been lost from their bodies. Traveling inside the tube, they cannot be seen and are safe from attack by enemies, such as birds, lizards, and ants.

Air-Conditioned Units

Huge colonies of termites in Africa live in air-conditioned homes built of soil. These termite buildings, known as mounds, have many different shapes and sizes. They can be more than 20 feet (6.1 meters) high and weigh several tons. The large mounds are only part of a colony's home—beneath the ground is a nest that is even more enormous.

Even the largest of these termite homes began as very small nests. To build their nest, a pair of mound-building termites, one male and one female, dig a vertical tunnel about 2 inches (5 centimeters) into the ground. They add a room, or chamber, by making the tunnel wider at the bottom. When they have finished, the two termites mate. Within a few weeks, the female begins laying eggs.

As more and more young termites hatch, the workers must keep making the nest larger. In the total darkness of their underground world, these insects build large, well-organized nests with many tunnels leading to many different rooms. The builders mix soil with their own sticky saliva to make a kind of plaster that holds the soil particles together and keeps the walls of the tunnels and rooms from falling in.

As the colony continues to grow, the termites begin expanding their home above the ground. The workers carry tiny bits of soil from their nest below ground to the new building site. They mix the soil with their saliva and put it in place. The mixture dries quickly and soon is strong and hard. The work continues, and a small mound of soil forms on top of the ground.

A huge termite mound bakes in the hot African sun.

As they are building the mound, these termite architects construct an incredible air-conditioning system that keeps air moving through their home. First, they dig a cellar just below the section of the nest that is underground. They leave several sturdy columns of soil in the cellar, however, to support the nest from below. Then, they construct several large tunnels leading from the cellar toward the outer walls of the mound. Sometimes, these large tunnels open to the outside.

MUSHROOM MOUNDS

Termite mounds are more than just piles of dirt. They are amazing buildings filled with activity. The king and queen of the colony live in a special underground "room" called the royal chamber or royal cell. They spend their lives there, and the queen continues laying as many as 30,000 eggs every day. During her lifetime—10 years or more—1 queen may produce more than 100 million eggs!

The workers clean and feed the royal pair, and carry the eggs from the royal chamber to the nursery rooms in other parts of the nest, where the eggs and the young are given special care. The termites also build rooms where they grow mushrooms in special gardens. The mushrooms grow on the moist surface of chewed wood and are used as food for the colony. Chewed wood that will eventually be cultivated in the mushroom gardens is kept in storage rooms nearby.

Next, the termites build a sturdy floor between the cellar and the bottom of the nest. The floor locks termites inside, but it also keeps dangerous enemies, such as ants, from entering the nest.

At the top of the mound, the builders leave an empty space, similar to an attic. This attic also has large tunnels that lead toward the walls of the mound, although they do not open to the outside. At the ends of the attic tunnels, just below the outer wall of the mound, the termites build large, flat rooms.

The air-conditioning system in this building is now ready to work. Heat is produced within the nest by the busy termites and by the decay of wood that is used to grow mushrooms. Because warm air is lighter than cooler air, the warm air rises up through the nest and into the attic. From there, the warm air flows through the attic tunnels to the large, flat rooms below the outer walls of the mound, where it seeps out through the porous walls.

INSIDE A TERMITE MOUND

Warm air radiates out through porous walls of mound.

Fresh air enters the mound through openings.

"Cultivated" mushroom gardens

Queen

Warm air rises.

Air falls as it is cooled inside.

As the warm air rises and leaves the nest, fresh air takes its place. This fresh air enters the building through the open tunnels and is cooled as it circulates inside the mound. The cooled air falls to the cellar, then passes up through the sturdy, but porous, cellar ceiling and into the nest. The fresh air brings oxygen into the nest for the termites to breathe; the rising warm air carries large amounts of carbon dioxide and other dangerous gases out of the nest.

As incredible as it may seem, some termites have developed another air-conditioning system to keep their homes comfortable. For this second system to work, however, the architects must change the shape of their mound a little. They add long, narrow ridges along the outside of the mound, from top to bottom. Within each of these ridges, there are many small tunnels that connect the attic to the cellar of the nest.

The warm air inside the nest rises into the attic and moves out along the ridges. Within the ridges, air is cooled slightly by the temperature outside of the mound. This cooled air then flows back into the cellar through the small tunnels in the ridges. As the air passes through the tunnels, fresh air with plenty of oxygen moves into the nest through the porous ridges. Carbon dioxide and other gases are forced through the walls and out of the mound.

Mound-building termites spend most of their lives sealed safely inside their sturdy homes. But without a good air-conditioning system, they would suffocate in just a few hours. Many animals build homes that last for only a few weeks or months. Some termite colonies, however, have lived in their homes for more than eighty years!

3

Wasps

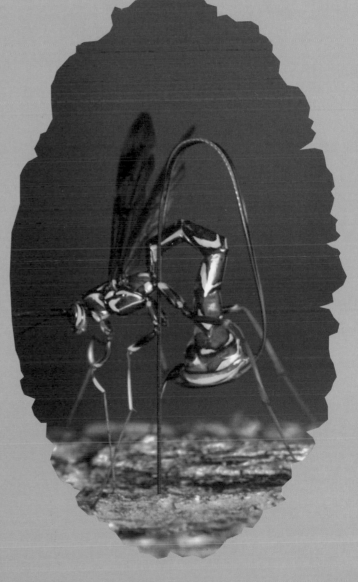

In Mexico, Brazil, and other places, people eat the honey that some wasps make. These insects, however, have given us much more than honey.

At the start of the eighteenth century, René-Antoine Ferchault de Réaumur, a French scientist, studied wasps at work, and learned how to use wood pulp to make paper. As a result, the paper made in many factories today is very similar to the paper that wasps make.

Female wasps are also very helpful to humans. Each year, while feeding their young, they kill millions of insect pests that damage food crops.

Wasps frighten many people who fear a painful sting. These insects, however, only use their stingers to protect themselves and their nest from harm. If they are left undisturbed, they will not bother humans.

HERE'S THE GRUB: WASP DEVELOPMENT

A wasp begins its life inside a small, whitish, oval-shaped egg. When the little insect hatches from the egg, it is a blind, hungry, worm-like larva (or grub). During this second stage of its life, it mostly eats insects that are captured and carried to the nest by adults.

After it grows to the proper size, the larva stops eating and spins a cocoon of silk around its body. The wasp, now called a pupa, remains almost motionless during this third stage of development. Its body, however, is still changing. Eventually, a fully developed adult wasp emerges from the cocoon and flies away. As adults, most wasps no longer eat insects. Instead, they drink the sweet, sugary nectar found in flowers.

Wasp pupae shown at various stages of development inside their cocoons.

The Houses that Wasps Build

There are 17,000 different kinds of known wasps. All adult wasps are either workers, queens, or males. The males, however, live for only a short time and die soon after mating. Therefore, most of the wasps we see are females, either queens or workers.

In the species known as solitary wasps, the females are all queens. They spend their lives alone, building nests and laying eggs. Other species are known as social wasps, and they live and work together in groups called colonies.

Wasps use mud in an ingenious way to construct a nest that holds a single egg. Some wasps make paper to build their amazing homes.

Starting the Nest

A wasp colony begins when a female builds her small nest and lays several eggs, from which more females emerge. Then the mother gathers food for her daughters until they are fully grown. The young adult wasps become workers. They make the nest larger, gather food, and raise the young. Their mother becomes the queen of the nest and continues laying eggs.

Toward the end of the summer, the queen lays more eggs, from which some male wasps emerge. The males later mate with females that were born at the same time. As winter approaches, the males die, but many of the females hibernate and survive the cold. They become next year's queens and build their first nests in the spring.

Pots of Clay

People are not the only creatures who make clay pots—and they weren't the first ones, either. In the insect world, potter wasps have been building clay, jug-shaped nests for millions of years.

Some people believe that the earliest Native Americans may have copied the shape of these wasp nests when making their first clay jars.

Before a female potter wasp can build her nest, she has two jobs to do. First, she must find a good, safe place to build her nest. She often chooses a place between two rocks or on the branch of a tree or bush. Next, she must find muddy soil that can be used to build the nest. If she can only find dry soil, she flies to find water and carries it in her stomach to the dry soil. She then spits the water onto the soil and makes her own mud!

Now, she can begin to construct the nest. Using her jaws and front pair of legs, the wasp architect rolls some mud into a small ball. She then carries the ball between her jaws to her building site. She presses the first few loads of mud flat against the rock or branch to form a round base, or floor.

Potter wasps use mud to create domed nests.

When the floor is finished, the wasp then begins building the walls of her nest. To do this, she sets a ball of mud along the edge of the floor. Using her legs, jaws, and abdomen, she pushes the mud into a thin, flat, narrow strip that reaches halfway around the floor. She presses another load of the mud into a flat strip around the other side of the floor. The first layer of

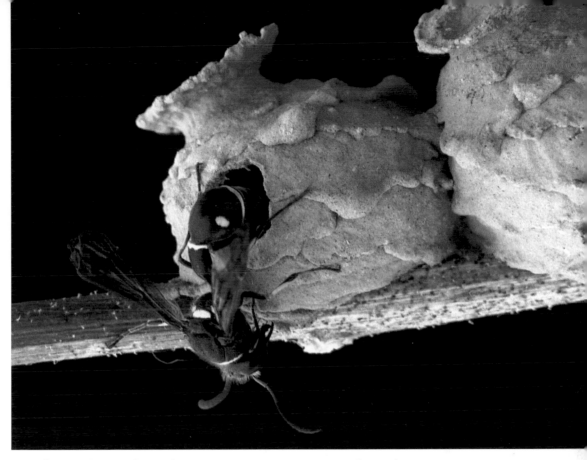

Two finished pot-shaped potter wasp nests sit on a branch.

the mud wall is now in place. While she works, she makes more balls of mud into thin, flat strips and presses them on top of each other, the wall gradually becomes higher. While the wasp is making the walls higher, she is also arching them together so that they form a mud dome.

The builder stops her work just before the dome is completed, leaving a small hole in the roof. It has taken the wasp almost two hours to build this nest, but her work is not yet done. Now, she must place an egg inside the little mud home. She inserts the rear end of her body through the roof hole and lays a tiny white egg. The egg has a thin thread attached at one end, which she uses to fasten the egg to the nest's ceiling.

A paralyzed spider is attached to the egg of a mud dauber wasp inside a chamber. **Inset**: The newly emerged larva feeds on the spider.

The mother wasp must now put some food in the nest. Soon, the egg will hatch, and a helpless, hungry larva will emerge, ready to eat. The potter now becomes a hunter in search of grubs or caterpillars, which she will push into the opening of her jug-shaped nest. The hunter does not kill her prey; she paralyzes it with a powerful sting. The grubs or caterpillars she captures remain alive, but unable to move. This way, when the larva hatches, it is able to eat fresh food.

After she has put a supply of food in the nest, the potter wasp mother has one more job to do. She carries a ball of mud to the nest and closes the hole in the roof, sealing her egg safely inside. The wasp then flies off to begin building another nest. She never sees the young wasp that will someday crawl from the little jug-shaped home she worked so hard to build.

Paper Homes

Many commonly seen wasp nests are actually made of paper. The builders—called paper wasps— even make the paper they use to construct their many-chambered homes. To do this, the insects scrape long, thin strips of wood from various objects—for example, unpainted boards or the stems of dry weeds. The wasps then roll the wood into balls and carry them to the building site, where they are mixed with the wasps' saliva and chewed into a paste called pulp. The pulp is then used to build a nest. When the pulp dries, it forms a strong, waterproof paper.

The color of a paper nest depends upon the color of the wood that was used to make it. Wasp nests are usually gray, because the little builders often make pulp from wood scraped from old fence posts and weathered barn boards.

Many wasp nests are made from paper produced by mixing chewed wood pulp with wasp saliva.

Field Wasps

Field wasps build some of the simplest paper nests, which are sometimes found under the branches of trees and bushes, but are more often seen under the eaves of houses or in barns, garages, and old sheds. The builders of these paper nests are the type of wasp that most people recognize.

When spring arrives, the field wasp is ready to begin raising her family. She mated the previous autumn and hibernated for the winter. After feeding on the sweet nectar of a few flowers, she sets out to find a good place to build her nest. She then finds a supply of wood to make the paper she needs.

To begin construction, she spreads a small dab of pulp at her building site. She adds more pulp to the center of this dab, shaping it into a thin, short stem about 1/2 inch (1.3 centimeters) long. Working from the tip of this sturdy little stem, the wasp begins building a small, shallow cup-shaped room called a cell. Using her jaws and legs, she forms the moist pulp into a thin paper wall. As more pulp is added to the lip of the cup, the cell becomes deeper.

This wasp is biting off some wood from a rotting log in order to make paper.

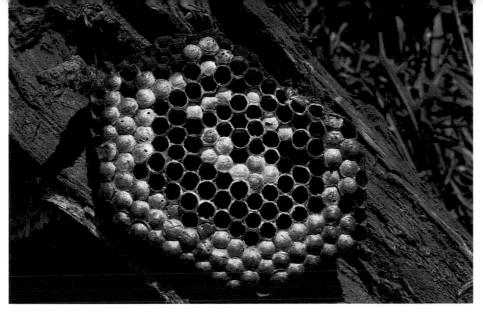

Many wasp nests are created from a series of six-sided (hexagonal) cells, each of which eventually contains an egg.

When she has finished, the wasp lays an egg in the cell. The egg is cemented securely to the wall. The wasp then begins building other cells around the first one in the same way. She lays one egg in each new cell as it is completed. This collection of six-sided (hexagonal) paper cells is called a comb.

The eggs begin to hatch about two weeks after they are laid. A wasp larva is blind and helpless and never leaves its small one-room cell. The mother wasp cares for her young, feeding them fresh grubs, caterpillars, and flower nectar. Within about two weeks, the larva grows into a pupa. During this time, the insect's body makes its final change. About three weeks later, an adult wasp crawls out of its cell and takes its place in the nest.

The mother wasp becomes the queen of the nest, and the young wasps—all females—become workers. The daughters feed developing larvae and make the nest larger. The queen lays eggs in the empty cells as the nest expands. By late summer, a large colony of field wasps may have as many as 200 adults living and working around one nest.

Hornets

The nests built by field wasps are very simple when compared to the nests of some hornets and yellowjackets. These insect architects build walls and roofs on their paper homes, so that their young are raised "indoors," protected from wind, rain, and dangerous enemies.

A female hornet, working alone, begins building her nest in the spring. Like her relative, the field wasp, she first builds a small, horizontal paper comb that has only a few cells. She then builds an umbrella-shaped roof over the comb and adds curved walls. After she has worked for about one week, the walls completely surround the comb. For entry and exit, the female leaves a small opening at the bottom of her golf-ball-sized paper nest.

Hornet nests are larger and heavier than those of most wasps, and are nearly fully enclosed.

The mother hornet lays an egg in each cell of her nest and cares for her young as they develop into adults. The young adult hornets—all female workers—quickly begin repairing the walls of the old comb, which were damaged as they hatched. They also work hard preparing to make the nest larger to accommodate the fast-growing colony.

Before the nest can be enlarged, however, the workers must remove part of the wall that surrounds the comb. After enlarging the comb, the workers must rebuild the wall of the nest. A worker sets a tiny dab of moist pulp along the edge of the nest wall. Then, she moves her head from side to side and, with her jaws, smears the pulp into a thin, curved strip. The moist pulp soon dries, forming a thin sheet of paper that has the swirled appearance seen in a finished nest. The workers add more dabs of pulp, until eventually a grayish-colored wall surrounds the combs of the enlarged nest.

The queen lays eggs in all the new cells, and soon new workers take their places within the colony. Again, parts of the wall are cut away so that the hornets' nest can become even larger. This time, however, the comb is repaired, but it is not made larger. Instead, a new comb is added below the original one to make room for the new insects.

Working near the center of the old comb, the hornets build a sturdy paper column and construct a small comb at the end of it. They are careful to allow just enough space so that they will be able to crawl between the two combs. They add more cells to the new comb and build more support columns as needed. The walls of the nest are rebuilt, and the hornets can now use both combs to raise their young. This process of building and repairing continues as the colony grows larger.

This hornet nest has three layers of combs—each time the nest is expanded a new comb is added below the old ones.

Throughout the summer, the workers enlarge their nest many times by cutting away parts of the wall around the combs, adding new combs below older ones, and rebuilding the walls. Some hornets' nests have more than ten combs built one above the other.

Each time the roof and walls of the nest are replaced, they become thicker because new pulp is being added to the layers of old paper. By the end of the summer, a colony with one queen may have grown to several thousand workers. These architects may have built a nest more than 1 foot (30 centimeters) wide, with walls 15 layers thick!

THE BUZZ IN THE UNDERGROUND

Although hornets often hang their nests in the branches of trees, some of their relatives build the same kind of nests underground. In the early spring,

the female yellowjacket looks for a tunnel that leads into the burrow (underground home) of a small animal. There, she builds her nest, attaching it to the roof of the burrow. As more and more workers join the colony, the nest is made larger.

These architects are not only papermakers, they are also miners. If the burrow becomes too small for their nest, the workers enlarge it by carrying soil up to the surface of the ground.

SOUTH AMERICAN SKYSCRAPERS

Hornets and yellowjackets may live in "high-rise" paper buildings, but some of their relatives in South America build "skyscrapers." Colonies of these fascinating tropical wasps build long, narrow, bell-shaped homes that hang beneath the branches of trees.

Working as a team, these architects construct a dome-shaped roof on the underside of a sturdy branch. Next, they build a floor beneath the roof by adding pulp around the bottom edges of the dome. Slowly, as load after load of moist pulp is put in place, the paper floor extends to fill the opening beneath the dome. The wasps then build a small paper comb below the floor.

When the first comb is finished, the wasps keep working to make their nest larger. They extend the edges of the dome-shaped roof a little farther and build another floor beneath the first one. Then, they build cells under the second floor to form another comb. Again, they extend the edges of the roof and build a floor and another comb.

As more floors are added, the nest gradually becomes larger. Some reach a finished length of more than 2 feet (61 centimeters) and have as many as 25 floors inside! These builders leave a small hole in the center of each floor so members of the colony can move throughout the entire nest to care for the young wasps in the cells of every comb.

Ants

Ants are probably the best-known insects in the world. They live in grassy fields and forests, in our backyards, and sometimes even in our homes. Ants live almost everywhere there is land, except in areas where it is always very cold.

Ants do a lot of useful work. They eat other insects, which helps control the insect population. Many of the insects that ants eat are harmful to gardens and to food crops. Also, when ants build their underground homes, they loosen the soil, allowing air and water to reach the roots of plants more easily.

Ants are unwelcome guests at picnics, but they are good to have around.

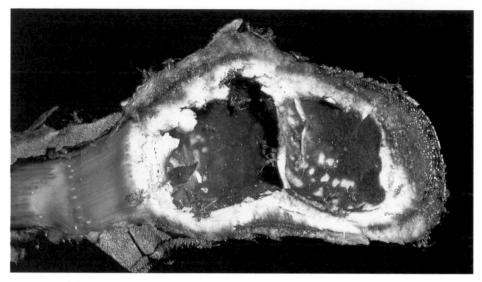

These Azteca ants in Peru live inside the hollow stem of a cecropia tree.

The Houses That Ants Build

Many of the 14,000 different species of ants build their homes underground. The kind of nest they construct, however, depends upon the specific kind of ants doing the work.

In some parts of the world, these insects live in huge mounds of twigs and soil that they pile on top of the ground. Some types of ants make their homes in wood or under the bark of trees. Others live in the hollow stems and thorns of plants. Some of the most fascinating ant nests are built with fresh leaves in treetops high above the ground.

Starting the Nest

Ants are known as social insects. Every ant is a member of a well-organized colony, and none of these insects lives alone. Although some species live in colonies with only 10 to 15 members, other species may live in colonies with more than 1 million ants!

Within an ant colony, there are three classes of ants—queens, males, and workers. The queens are the only female ants that are able to lay eggs, and they continue to lay eggs for as long as they live. The males' only job is to mate with the queens. A short time after mating, the male ants die. Most of the ants we see are female workers. Their job is to care for the queen, raise the young, find food, enlarge the nest, and defend the nest against invaders.

Workers in a red wood ant nest carry larvae from the breeding chambers.

After mating, a young queen begins looking for a place to live. She either joins an existing colony or she starts a colony of her own. To start a colony, the female must build a small nest in which to lay her first batch of tiny eggs. The queen cares for her young until they become adults, at which time they take their places as worker ants within the colony.

Giant Anthills

In forests throughout much of Europe and Asia, colonies of red wood ants build huge dome-shaped homes that are sometimes more than 6 feet (2 meters) high. These enormous anthills are impressive enough on the outside—but this is only the "upstairs" section of the ants' home. Red wood ants also build thousands of tunnels and rooms in the soil below the anthill. The "downstairs" section of the nest may extend as deep under the ground as the top of the anthill stands above it.

A large wood ant nest may have more than 1 million workers and several hundred queens living inside. When the nest becomes too crowded, some of the queens leave, each taking several thousand workers with her. These small groups of ants do not travel far, however, before the workers begin building their queens' new homes.

A colony of red wood ants often builds its nest in a rotten tree stump. The workers can easily dig tunnels and build rooms in the soft wood. If they cannot find an old, rotting stump, however, the workers tunnel into the soil. They dig several small holes by carrying tiny clumps of dirt to the surface of the ground in their jaws. The workers then tunnel through the soil to connect the holes and create underground passageways.

They add rooms to their nest by enlarging sections of the tunnels. Soon, the colony has a small new home.

Once the colony is safe within its new nest, the workers conceal all the "door" openings that lead into it to protect themselves from enemies. They pile pieces of leaves, grasses, pine needles, mosses, twigs, and other vegetation on top of the openings. As more and more material is added to the pile, the anthill gradually grows higher. Many of the workers do not carry their loads all the way to the top. Instead, they drop them along the sides, which makes the pile rounded or dome-shaped. Because of its shape, this type of anthill is often called a mound nest.

The wood ant architects also add rooms and passageways within the mound. As the mound becomes larger, more and more rooms and tunnels are added.

A RED ANT ANTHILL

Workers are constantly bringing damp, rotting materials to the outside.

Workers carry materials such as grasses, pine needles, and other vegetation to the anthill to build up the outside and cover openings.

Certain workers remain inside to care for developing larvae and to tend the queen.

A rotten tree stump is often found at the anthill's center.

Hundreds of connected chambers and passageways are made, both above and below ground.

Even though the doors to the nest are safely concealed under vegetation, the ants can move in and out of the mound through small openings in the surface. Workers pass through these hard-to-find doors to gather more building materials and food for the ants inside the nest.

While some ants are building the mound higher, others are making the nest below ground larger, too. The workers build new rooms and tunnels, gather food, and take care of the young ants. The queen continues laying eggs. When the eggs hatch and more workers join the colony, the nest is made larger.

The red wood ants' nest is a busy place. Each day, workers are busy carrying pieces of grass, leaves, tiny twigs, and other materials from inside the mound to the outside. To us, this may seem like a waste of time, but it is not. Because of the warm temperature and the moist air created by the breathing of thousands of ants, the building materials that are deep within the mound become damp. If these damp materials were not brought to the surface to dry in the sun, they would become covered with molds and rot away. The molds would quickly destroy the mound of vegetation, and the wood ants' home would be ruined. Because of the ants' hard work, some mounds have lasted for more than sixty years!

The temperature within one of these large ant homes is about 77° Fahrenheit (25° Centigrade) most of the time. During the day, the mound is warmed by the sun. If, however, more heat is needed deep within the nest, hundreds or thousands of ants come out of the mound and stand in the sun warming their bodies. When they crawl back inside, they carry a little heat with them, and other ants go out to soak up more heat from the sun. At night, when the temperature outside the nest drops, the ants keep the heat inside their home by blocking the doors or entrance holes that lead from the nest. During very cold winter months, the ants move into the deepest parts of their underground home, where the temperatures are the warmest. There, the colony can survive until spring.

The shape and design of the red wood ants' mound also helps to keep the ants dry. Because of the mound's steep slope, rainwater rolls off quickly. Although the warmth of the sun soaks into the mound, falling rain cannot seep through the tightly packed bits of vegetation.

LITTLE BIG EATERS

A colony of 1 million red wood ants needs an enormous amount of food. They are, by necessity, excellent hunters. Each day, the workers must kill about 100,000 small insects, such as flies, beetle grubs, caterpillars, and butterflies. Many of the insects that these ants eat are harmful to the crops that humans grow. Because of this, many people have traditionally used red wood ants to control insect pests. These valuable ants are even protected by law in some parts of the world.

A swarm of red wood ants attacks a beetle.

Woven Tree Houses

Some of the most unusual ant houses in the world are built by weaver ants. These ants are found in tropical forests around the world. They live in trees, not in the soil like many of their relatives. To build their homes, these ant architects actually sew fresh leaves together with threads of silk.

First, a female weaver ant finds a leaf high in a tree on which to lay her eggs. Her small batch of eggs is attached securely to the healthy leaf she chooses. Then, she waits. The worm-like larvae that emerge from the eggs change into pupae and then into adult worker ants. The queen continues laying eggs while the young workers hunt for food, raise the next batch of young, and build shelters in which to live.

When a colony of weaver ants is ready to build their tree-top home, the workers search for two healthy leaves that are growing close together. When a worker is able to pull two leaves toward one another, other workers rush to help. The group of ants quickly forms a line along the edge of one leaf. Clinging tightly to the leaf with the claws of their six feet, the workers reach out and grasp the second leaf firmly in their powerful jaws. By walking backward, the ants slowly pull the edges of the leaves together.

Sometimes, the leaves are too far apart for the ants to reach between them—but help soon arrives. While one ant is stretching to reach the second leaf, another worker crawls over that ant, stretches even further, and grabs the leaf. The first ant then closes its jaws firmly around the narrow waist of its helper, and the two ants form a living chain to bridge the gap. If the space between the leaves is still too wide, other workers join the chain until the job is done.

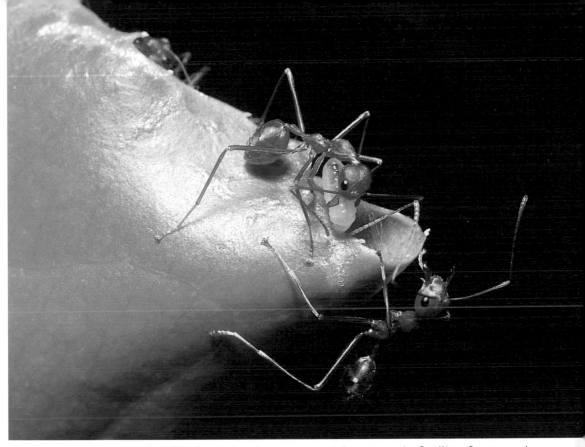

A weaver ant worker holds a larva in place as a sticky strand of silk is fastened to the leaves of the nest.

When the two leaves have been pulled together, another group of workers sews their edges with threads of silk. Adult ants cannot make silk, but the developing larvae produce a sticky liquid that quickly dries into a thin, silk thread.

Workers carry larvae in their jaws to the building site. They place a larva's head on one of the leaves and use their antennae signals to stimulate the larva to produce a thread of silk. While the thread is being made, the worker carries the larva over to the second leaf. The worker pushes the larva's head down onto that leaf, and the silk thread is again attached. This process creates the first stitch. The worker continues carrying the larva back and forth between the two leaves, and a strand of silk is laid down with each crossing. At the same time, other workers, holding larvae in their jaws, are stitching together different sections of the leaves in the same way, until a thick web of silk fastens both leaves together along one edge.

The workers then pull the opposite edges of the two leaves together. They sew those edges to form the weaver ants' tent-like tree house. If a leaf is large enough, the ants may simply fold it in half and sew around the edges, rather than stitching it to a second leaf.

ANT-I PEST

Weaver ants are vicious hunters that allow few other insects to live in their trees. Even a weaver ant from another colony that wanders up the wrong tree is quickly killed and eaten.

Because of their excellent hunting skills, weaver ants have been used for centuries in China to control insect pests in citrus trees. To move the ants to where they are needed, the Chinese wrap a cloth around the nest before cutting it down. The nest is then hung in the tree that needs protection, and the wrap is removed. Soon, the pests are under control.

Weaver ants are fierce hunters and defenders of their nests. Here, a team of ants attack an intruding caterpillar.

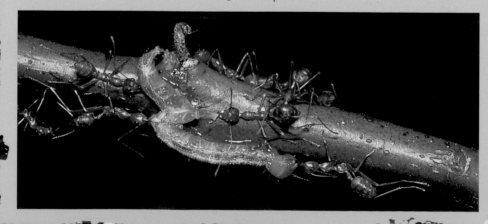

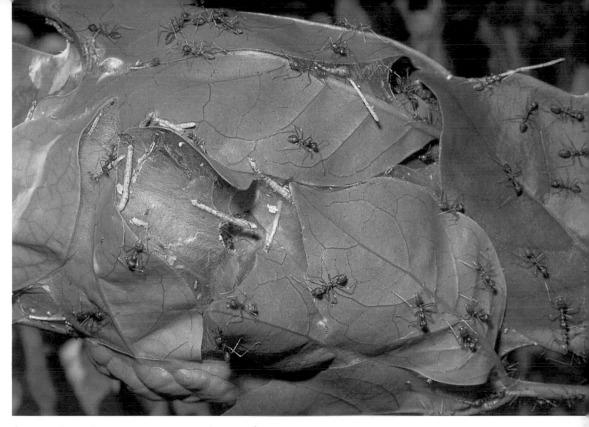

A completed weaver ant nest hangs from a tree.

Within the nest, the weaver ants also build tunnels and chambers with silk and leaves. From start to finish, these insects need about twenty-four hours to build a leafy, treetop home. The nest will last for more than one month, and then a new one must be built.

Only a small, new colony of weaver ants can live in a single nest. As the number of ants in the colony increases, the ants build more nests. Some large colonies have more than 1 million weaver ants living in more than 150 nests. A colony of this size, however, does not build all of its houses in just one tree. The ants may have nests in more than twenty different trees, within an area of forest the size of half a football field. This is a very large living area for an ant whose body is less than 1/2 inch (1.3 centimeters) long!

Bees

When most people hear the word "bee," they think of those busy little insects that make the honey we eat. Although honeybees are probably the most famous type of bee, they have many interesting relatives. About 20,000 different kinds of bees can be found on Earth— from the hot, steamy tropics to some cold polar regions. The smallest of these insects is barely 1/13 inch (2 millimeters) long. The largest bees have a body length of more than 1 inch (25 millimeters).

All bees have a special relationship with the flowers that live nearby. A bee's only source of food is the pollen and sweet liquid nectar that flowers produce. In return, bees help the plants to survive and reproduce. For plants to reproduce, it is often necessary for their pollen to travel between flowers. As a bee goes from flower to flower gathering food, it drops tiny bits of pollen collected from one flower into the next one it visits. In this way, bees play an important role in plant pollination. Many plants have bright, beautiful flowers that attract the bees and entice them to land. Once they do, they collect pollen on their hairy legs before buzzing off to the next flower and depositing some of the dusty material there.

The Houses That Bees Build

Most people think of bees as living in large colonies and working together to make wax combs filled with honey. This is true only for certain types of bees, such as the well-known honeybees and the larger, often-seen bumblebees. These bees are social insects that work together and cooperate in order to survive. Most bees, however, spend their lives working alone. They are known as solitary bees.

There are two interesting architects in the world of bees. The first is the carpenter bee, which works alone. Instead of hammers and saws, carpenter bees use different parts of their bodies as their tools. They build their safe, sturdy homes by tunneling into wood.

The second architect is a type of bumblebee that builds a honeycomb nest of wax. Bumblebees begin work alone, but soon get help.

A carpenter bee winds its way through a tunnel it has burrowed out of wood.

Starting the Nest

In a colony of social bumblebees, most of the individuals are females, either queens or workers. The male bees, called drones, have only one job. In the fall, they mate with the young, future queens. Soon after mating, the males die, and the females find a safe place to hibernate for the winter.

In the warmth of the spring sunshine, the female bumblebees begin building their nests and laying eggs to start their families. When the first batch of eggs hatches, the worker bees take over the running of the nest. The queen continues to lay eggs and is cared for by her young.

Life is a little different for the solitary carpenter bees. During the cold winter months, both the male and female bees hibernate in their nests, which are built in wood.

When spring arrives, carpenter bees become active. They spend their days feeding on the sweet nectar of spring flowers. When they have regained their strength, they clean out and enlarge their old nests. After mating, the female works alone to prepare a nest for her eggs. In late August, the old bees die, and the next generation emerges from the nest—without ever meeting their parents.

Wood Tunnels

Building a home and nursery is the job of each female carpenter bee. To begin, she finds a piece of wood in a protected place that is well lit and warmed by the sun.

Carpenter bees most often build their homes in pine, redwood, cypress, and cedar, although they may inhabit other types of wood. They do not use wood that is painted or has bark on it, so their homes are usually found in logs, fence posts, poles, or the unpainted wooden parts of houses—such as doors, windowsills, and rafters.

Once a female carpenter bee finds a good place to build, she uses her sharp, powerful jaws to cut her way inside the wood. As she tunnels in, she makes a

Carpenter bees cut L-shaped tunnel-homes for themselves in fence posts, logs, and other unpainted wooden structures.

perfectly round hole about 1/2 inch (1.3 centimeters) in diameter. Usually, the bee enters the wood by cutting across the grain. To do this, she must chew her way through rings of soft, light wood, but also through rings of harder, dark wood. This is difficult work, and it goes slowly.

After 2 days, she has dug her way 1 inch (2.5 centimeters) into the wood. On the third day, however, she does not continue tunneling in a straight line. Instead, she changes direction, boring sharply to the left or right to follow the wood's grain. Because she is now cutting with the grain, the work is easier and goes much faster. She continues working until she has dug a tunnel that is 1/2 inch (1.3 centimeters) wide and 4 to 6 inches (10 to 15 centimeters) long. When she is done, the bee has a sturdy wooden L-shaped house.

"Bee Bread"

The busy female must now gather food for the young bees that will soon be growing in her nest. She collects dry, powdery pollen and liquid, sugary nectar from nearby flowers and mixes them together. The mixture becomes a dough-like "bee bread."

The bee puts a small loaf of this bread—about the size of a large jelly bean—at the end of the tunnel farthest from the opening. She then lays a single egg on top of the food. The female bee uses tiny bits of chewed wood and saliva to build a thin wall, which seals the bread in with her first egg. It takes one day to prepare this first cell. She builds one cell each day for five more days, until six cells, positioned one next to the other, line the tunnel.

With her work completed, the female bee rests and dies before her young develop in the safety of their home. When the first egg hatches in the late summer, a blind, legless larva (or grub) emerges and begins eating its supply of bread. After five to seven weeks, the bee is a fully developed adult.

Not all bees need exactly the same amount of time to develop, which means that the first egg laid does not always produce the first adult bee. Whichever bee develops first chews its way through the walls that separate the cells, crawls over its undeveloped brothers and sisters, and leaves the nest. Usually, all of the young bees leave the nest within just a few days. Once outside, with the mother gone, they must care for themselves and go off in search of food.

Hibernation

The new adults do not travel far from home. They spend much of their time gathering and eating pollen and nectar from flowers they visit. As summer passes and the weather becomes cold, the bees crawl back into their nest and hibernate. They spend the winter inside, lined up head to tail, facing away from the entrance hole. Carpenter bees that live in places with warm weather year-round do not hibernate; they simply continue their nesting activities uninterrupted.

Hibernating bees become active again in the spring when the temperature rises and stays at about 75° Fahrenheit (24° Centigrade). They leave the nest tunnel and again feed on the sweet, sugary nectar of the flowers. Within a few weeks, the bees mate, and the females begin preparing nests in which to lay their eggs.

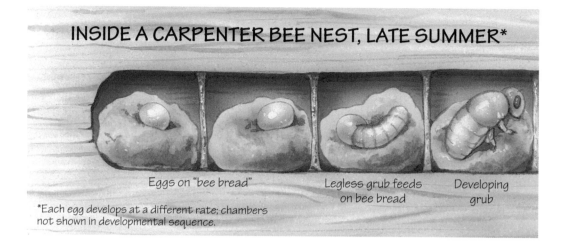

INSIDE A CARPENTER BEE NEST, LATE SUMMER*

Eggs on "bee bread"

Legless grub feeds on bee bread

Developing grub

*Each egg develops at a different rate; chambers not shown in developmental sequence.

A female carpenter bee may either dig a new tunnel or use the old nest that her mother or another female bee built. If an old nest is used, she cleans it out, pushing debris to the ground below. Then, she is ready to begin making bread and laying eggs in the nest. Some females make the old nest tunnel longer. When the same homes are used for a long time, the nest tunnels can become 6 to 10 feet (2 to 3 meters) long. Scientists found one nest in Missouri that was thought to be in constant use for fourteen years!

Houses of Wax

Of all the different kinds of bees, the large, hairy, black-and-yellow bumblebee is one of the best known and most often seen. There are more than 200 species of these insects, and most live in the temperate (mild) regions of Europe, Asia, and North America. Some make their homes near the equator—where it is very hot—or in the cold climates near the North and South poles.

Grub

At 5 to 7 weeks, the bee is fully developed

Mother dies after eggs are laid

The female bumblebee—the queen—crawls from her winter hiding place, hungry and ready to raise a family. After feeding on a few spring flowers, she begins looking for a good place to build her nest. She tries to find an abandoned burrow that was built by a small mammal, such as a mouse, chipmunk, or shrew. Her search may take a few days or even a few weeks.

When she has found the right spot, she goes to work. She pushes and pulls her way through the dry grasses that had been used as soft bedding by the nest's original owner. The bee makes a short tunnel, and at the end of it, a small room about 1 inch (2.5 centimeters) high and 1 inch wide.

The queen may then cover the ceiling and walls of the room with wax to keep the moisture from the ground out of her nest. This wax is secreted by special glands and collects on the surface of the bee's abdomen, where it forms small, thin flakes. The bee removes these flakes of wax with her legs, places them between her jaws, and chews them until the wax is soft enough to mold into shape.

Small clumps of pollen are deposited in the single cells of this bumblebee nest.

The female next prepares a place to lay her eggs. With wax, she builds a small, shallow bowl on the floor of the nest. When the bowl is ready, the bee gathers pollen from the flowers and carries it on her hind legs to the nest. When she rubs her hind legs together, the load of pollen is dumped onto the nest floor. The queen shapes the pollen into a ball and places it in her wax bowl. She then lays from eight to fourteen eggs on the pollen. Afterwards, she builds a dome-shaped roof of wax over the bowl to form a hollow, ball-shaped cell full of eggs.

After the first batch of eggs hatch, the larvae begin eating the pollen in the ball underneath them. This food lasts only a short time, however, so the queen must collect more pollen. To feed her young, she uses her jaws to cut a slit through the roof of their wax egg cell. She drops a "bee bread" of honey and pollen into the cell next to the larvae and then seals the slit shut again with more wax.

LIKE HONEY TO THE BEE

While the queen bumblebee is building the cell for her egg, she is also making plans for a rainy day. Out of wax, she makes a honey pot that is about the size of a thimble. She builds the pot just inside the entrance to the nest and fills it with honey. This way, she has food to eat during bad weather when she cannot leave the nest.

A bumblebee honey pot, made from wax, sits next to a clump of egg packets in a nest.

As the bees grow, the wax egg cell around them gradually expands. While in the cell, each fully developed larva spins a cocoon of silk around its body. After the cocoon is formed, the queen breaks apart the cell's wax walls. Within its own silk blanket, the larva gradually changes into a pupa. Finally, it emerges from the cocoon as an adult bumblebee. The complete change from egg to adult takes about three weeks.

The bees from these first eggs are all female workers and do not lay eggs. Instead, they enlarge the nest, build new egg cells, gather pollen and nectar, care for the next batch of developing young, and defend the nest. Workers only live about two weeks. They are replaced by the younger sisters that they helped to raise.

During the summer, the queen spends much of her time laying more eggs to produce more female workers. The family of bumblebees soon becomes larger and larger, and as many as 300 to 400 workers might be found sharing one nest.

Bumblebee eggs sit on top of a clump of nectar and pollen "bread," which will provide food for newly hatched grubs.

Bumblebees collect pollen from flowers to make food packets for newly hatched larvae.

As the end of summer approaches, the queen begins laying eggs that will produce males to be next year's drones and the females that will be next year's queens. When these males and future queens become adults, they leave the nest and fly away in search of mates.

Soon after mating, females crawl into underground tunnels to hibernate for the winter. In temperate and cold climates, these female bumblebees are the only bees that survive until the following spring. Their mother, sisters, and mates, having done their jobs, die during the fall, as the days become shorter and colder. The new queens spend the winter in a deep sleep beneath the ground, waiting for the warmer days of spring when they will build a home and raise a family, just as their mother did the year before.

Classification Chart of Termites, Wasps, Ants, and Bees

Within the animal kingdom, all animals with similar characteristics are separated into a smaller group called a phylum. Similar animals within a phylum are next separated into even smaller groups known as classes. Then, the similar animals of a class are separated into smaller groups called orders. The orders are divided into families.

The following chart provides information about the phylum, class, and order of the insects discussed in this book.

Classification	General Description	Examples	Number of Species
KINGDOM: Animalia		All animals	More than 1,000,000
PHYLUM: Arthropoda	Segmented body (separate body divisions) with a hard covering. Appendages with joints.	Centipedes, ticks, lobsters, spiders, insects	More than 840,000
CLASS: Insecta	Three body parts: head, thorax (chest), and abdomen. Three pairs of legs and usually two pairs of wings. Head has one pair of antennae.	All insects	More than 700,000
ORDER: Isoptera	Two pairs of wings when present; both pairs look similar. Chewing mouth parts.	Termites	More than 3,000
ORDER: Hymenoptera	Two pairs of transparent wings when present; front wings larger than hind wings. Chewing or sucking mouth parts.	Ants, bees, wasps	More than 100,000
SUPERFAMILY: Apoidea	Stocky body covered with some hairs that branch.	Bees	More than 20,000
Vespoidea	Body thinner than body of bee. Unbranching hairs on body.	Potter wasps, paper wasps, hornets, yellowjackets	More than 17,000
Formicoidea	One or two knots (or lumps) on the thin waist between thorax and abdomen. Antennae elbowed.	Ants	More than 14,000

Common Names and Scientific Names

All plants and animals have formal Latin names. Many also have common names, or nicknames. The formal name of a plant or animal is called the scientific name, and it is the same all over the world. A common name, however, can be different from place to place and in different languages.

Common names can sometimes be confusing because different kinds of plants or different kinds of animals may have the same common name. For example, if someone said that they saw a trap-door spider, you could not be certain whether it was the spider that builds simple tube-like homes, the one that builds wishbone-shaped burrows, or the one that builds burrows with side doors.

In the chart below, you will find the common name (nickname) and the scientific name (formal name) for each insect discussed in this book. Each scientific name has two parts.

The first part, called the genus, always begins with a capital letter. The genus includes the small group of animals that are similar to one another in many ways.

The second part of the scientific name, called the species, is not capitalized. The species includes animals that are exactly alike. If the exact species is not known, then the genus name is given alone.

Common Name or Type of Nest	Scientific Name	Common Name or Type of Nest	Scientific Name
Termites		**Ants**	
Eastern subterranean termite	*Reticulitermes flavipes*	Red wood ant	*Formica rufa*
Mound-building termite*	*Macrotermes bellicosus*	Weaver ant	*Oecophylla longinoda*
Wasps		**Bees**	
Potter wasp	*Eumenes fraternus*	Carpenter bee	*Xylocopa virginica*
Paper wasps:		Bumblebee	*Bombus lapidarius*
Field wasp	*Polistes fuscatus*		
Bald-faced hornet	*Vespula maculata*		
Yellowjacket	*Vespula maculifrons*		
Tropical wasp	*Chartergus chartarius*		

This insect has no common name

59

Glossary

abdomen (AB-duh-muhn) The rear section of an arthropod.

arthropod (AHR-thruh-pahd) A member of the largest animal group, belonging to the phylum Arthropoda (AHR-thruh-po-duh). These animals have no backbones and have legs with joints. Insects, spiders, and crustaceans are examples of arthropods.

burrow A hole in the ground where an animal lives, hides, and raises its young.

chamber An enclosed space, such as a cave, room, or cell.

cocoon (kuh-KOON) A covering that protects the pupae of many insects, often made of silk.

colony A group of animals of the same kind living together.

comb A group of compartments, or cells, built by bees or wasps, in which honey and pollen are stored and the young insects develop.

decompose To decay or to separate into basic parts.

hibernate (HI-bur-naht) To spend the winter in a sleep-like state.

horizontal In a position parallel to the horizon.

juvenile Young or immature individual.

larva (LAHR-vah) (plural: larvae [LAHR-vye]) The worm-like insect that hatches from the egg.

metamorphosis (meht-uh-MAWR-fuh-sihs) The change that an insect undergoes as it hatches from its egg and develops into an adult.

nymph (NIMF) A termite in its early stages of life, between hatching from its egg and becoming an adult.

phylum (FY-luhm) (plural: phyla [FY-LA]) A large group of plants or animals; one of the primary divisions of the plant and animal kingdoms.

pollination (pahl-uh-NA-shun) The transfer of pollen from the anther (the male part of a flower) to the stigma (the female part of a flower).

porous (POR-uhs) Having many tiny holes within a dense surface through which air or liquids can pass.

prey (PRAY) An animal that is hunted, killed, and eaten by another animal.

pulp (PUHLP) A soft, moist mixture of plant fibers used to make paper.

pupa (PYOO-puh) (plural: pupae [PYOO-pay]) The stage after the larval stage in an insect's life, before it becomes an adult. A caterpillar in its cocoon is a pupa.

saliva A liquid produced in the mouth that helps in swallowing and digesting food.

scientific name The two-part Latin name given to every different kind, or species, of plant and animal. Every species has its own scientific name; in this way, a plant or animal that has more than one common name can be properly identified worldwide.

social Describes animals that live in an organized group.

solitary Describes animals that live alone.

species (SPEE-seez) A single category of plant or animal with common char-acteristics.

subterranean (sub-tuh-ray-NE-uhn) Underground.

termitarium (tur-mih-TAIR-ee-uhm) (plural: termitaria) A termite nest or home.

temperate (TEM-puhr-it) The areas of Earth that have a climate that is warm in summer, cold in winter, and moder-ate in the spring and fall.

Source Notes

Behnke, Frances L. *A Natural History of Termites*. New York: Charles Scribner's Sons, 1977.

Burton, Maurice. *Insects and Their Relatives*. New York: Facts on File, 1984.

Cole, Joanna. *An Insect's Body*. New York: William Morrow and Company, 1984.

Fischer-Nagel, Heiderose. *Life of the Honeybee*. Minneapolis: Carolrhonda Books, 1982.

Graham, Ada, and Graham, Frank. *Busy Bugs*. New York: Dodd, Mead and Compnay, 1983.

Greenland, Caroline. *Ants*. Danbury, Conn.: Grolier, 1985.

Horton, Casey. Insects. New York: Gloucester Press, 1984.

Hutchins, Ross E. *Paper Hornets*. Reading, Mass.: Addison-Wesley Publishing Co., 1973.

Hutchins, Ross E. *Insects and Their Young*. New York: Dodd, Mead and Company, 1975.

Johnson, Sylvia A. *Wasps*. Minneapolis: Lerner Publications, 1984.

Kelsey, Elin. *Bees*. New York: Grolier Educational Corporation, 1985.

Kohn, Bernice. *The Busy Honeybee*. New York: Four Winds Press, 1972.

Limburg, Peter R. *Termites*. New York: Hawthorn Books, 1974.

Nanao, Jun. *Life of the Ant*. Milwaukee: Raintree Publishers, 1986.

Norsgarad, Ernestine J. *Insect Communities.* New York: Grosset and Dunlap, 1973.

O'Toole, Christopher. *Discovering Bees and Wasps.* New York: The Bookwright Press, 1986.

Overbeck, Cynthia. *Ants.* Minneapolis: Lerner Publications Company, 1982.

Owen, Jennifer. *Mysteries and Marvels of Insect Life.* London: Usborne Publishing, 1984.

Parker, Nancy Winslow, and Joan Richards Wright. *Bugs.* New York: Greenwillow Books, 1987.

Pitt, Valerie, and David Cook. *A Closer Look at Ants.* New York: Franklin Watts, 1975.

Reigot, Betty, P. *Questions and Answers About Bees.* New York: Scholastic, 1983.

For More Information

Books

Brenner, Barbara. Carol Schwartz. *Thinking About Ants.* Greenvale, NY: Mondo Publishing, 1997.

Hunt, Joni Phelps. Vicki Leon (Editor). *Insects: All About Ants, Aphids, Bees, Fleas, Termites, Toebiters & a Beetle or Two* (Close Up). Morristown, NJ: Silver Burdett Press, 1995.

Johnson, Sylvia A. Nick Von Ohlen. *A Beekeeper's Year.* Boston, MA: Little, Brown & Co., 1994.

Johnson, Sylvia A. Hiroshi Ashinagabachi Ogawa (Photographer). *Wasps.* Minneapolis, MN: Lerner Publications Co., 1984.

Pascoe, Elaine. Dwight Kuhn (Photographer). *Ants* (Nature Close-Up). Woodbridge, CT: Blackbirch Press, Inc., 1999.

Telford, Carole. Rod Theodorou. *Through A Termite City.* Des Plaines, IL: Heinemann, 1998.

Web Sites

Bee Alert!
Discover facts about these interesting insects with bee trivia, learn what famous people were beekeepers, and view the live bee cam to see what is going on in the hive today—
biology.dbs.umt.edu/bees/kids.htm.

Dr. Don's Termite Page
See unusual photographs and find out strange termite facts as you learn about the ecology and behavior of the insects—
www.labyrinth.net.au/~dewart/directory.htm#nowhere.

Index

Photo Credits
Cover: (top termites) ©Patti Murray/Animals Animals, (bottom left) ©PhotoDisc, (top and bottom right bees) ©Corel Corporation; pages 3, 6, 8, 10, 18, 21, 30, 35, 41 (background), 46, 57: ©Corel Corporation; page 11: ©C.C. Lockwood/Animals Animals; pages 12, 14, 33: ©Raymond Mendez/ Animals Animals; page 13: ©Patti Murray/Animals Animals; page 15: ©Nigel Smith/Animals Animals; page 17: ©Michael & Barbara Reed/Animals Animals; pages 22, 27, 28, 32, 37, 41: ©Hans Pfletschinger/Peter Arnold; pages 24, 43, 45: ©K.G. Preston-Mafham/Peter Arnold; page 25: ©Maria Zorn/Animals Animals; page 26: ©Bill Beatty/Animals Animals; page 29: ©Perry Slocum/ Animals Animals; page 36: ©Michael Doolittle/Peter Arnold; page 44: ©W.F. Mantis/OSF/Animals Animals; page 48: ©Brent P. Kent/Animals Animals; pages 54-56: ©D. Shale/OSF/Animals Animals.

Illustration Credits
Pages 7, 9: ©Michael Felber; pages 19, 34, 39, 49, 52–53: ©Carlyn Iverson/Absolute Science.